Forming a View

The Art of Thinking

Secrets of being effective in the
world of business and investments

An Apprentice

DEDICATION

This book is dedicated to all those who take action and
prepare themselves to become better in what they do

CONTENTS

ACKNOWLEDGMENTS

I would like to acknowledge my dearest family, my parents,
my mentors and colleagues who have taught me
countless things and life's lessons.
Special thanks to the entrepreneurial thought leaders,
investment legends and business icons who have inspired
and continue to inspire me greatly all these years.

1 INTRODUCTION

First and foremost, I would like to congratulate you for taking the initiative to pick up this book. I can only speculate why the reader will pick up this book. Is it because of the title "Forming a View"? Does this title resonate with you, the reader? Or do you, like many practitioners of the corporate world, simply wish to unravel the mystery behind this critically important skill known as "Forming Views"? The world of business finance and investments is a highly fluid and competitive environment, yet it is this very aspect of the industry that makes it alluring to many people seeking to find new intellectually stimulating challenges. This is a world where one needs to understand the key value drivers of a business or industry and make sound decisions based on that understanding. Therefore, the ability to form views, efficiently and effectively, becomes a critical stepping stone for success in this industry. Yet it is not a skill that one can develop in an instant, though knowing where to start will save one from a painful and arduous journey fraught with self-doubt and self-criticism[1].

How often are we asked to form a view about a company, a situation, an opportunity or a person in the course of our work? As we strive to find a role in this knowledge-based economy, it seems like we need to form a view about practically anything and everything. With the advent of incredible search engines such as Google and Bing[2] along with the revolution of highly personalized and portable mobile devices, it is no longer the exclusive access to information that helps us form views. With a simple mouse click, or the touch from the tip of one's finger on a smart-phone, or even the voice command to a Personal Digital Assistant such as "Siri"[3] on the iPhone, anyone can get access to information readily and efficiently.

---

[1] Veteran investment practitioners and traders will often tell you how operating within "the Market" can be a very humbling experience, because even the best among them will encounter times where their views are proven wrong.

[2] Bing is the search engine developed by Microsoft

[3] Siri is the personal digital assistant developed by Apple for the Iphone series

In the past, he who can get hold of information fastest will be the delight of his stakeholders – his superiors, bosses, or customers, but those were the days when digital technology and the internet were at their nascent development stage. Bosses and customers require the knowledge operators of today to generate insights from whatever information they can get. Mere access to information means absolutely nothing in this hyper-connected world. It is often what we do with what we know that makes all the difference. The cutting edge is about speed and accuracy of the views and consequently, the decisions made. Therefore, forming views is a skill, a skill that needs to be honed through practice and experience.

Yet, how often do we experience and observe indecisiveness? For all the tools that we learnt in school and in the professional workplace, why is it that we see some folks who are very efficient in getting the information they need and consequently, effective in forming accurate views; but yet at the same time, we also suffer under many more who are just "all-over-the-place" and cannot feel convicted in whatever opinions they have? In fact, I would argue that examples of analysis-paralysis syndrome is abundant everywhere and causes much unnecessary distress for both the managers and the managed.

As such, it is my sincere goal to embark on a journey to document what I have learnt and observed over the last decade working in the investment world, and to help the newcomers in this exciting world of business and investments to jump-start the process, but before that, let me explain what this book is NOT. This is strictly not a technical How-To book, and this is most certainly not a Get-Rich-Quick book, with a panacea to solve all the problems one would face in the corporate and investments world. This is a book that seeks to show you a path towards becoming more effective in the business and investments world by introducing you to approach any challenges with a fresh perspective.

As Morpheus from the classic movie for geeks, The Matrix (1999) said: *"I'm trying to free your mind, Neo. But I can only show you the door. You're the one that has to walk through it."*

A mentor of mine once told me, "if you can get one good idea from a book, then it is a good book." In this book, I will attempt to give you 2 good ideas. These 2 ideas, upon internalization, will allow you to form intelligent views effectively. More specifically, I will illustrate how a greenhorn to the corporate world can benefit greatly from these 2 ideas. In fact, corporate veterans will find this book a good refresher on how to navigate the waters of the business and investments world.

Writing a book on forming views can be very ambitious, because there are so many things in the world that we can form views on. However, you will find that this book is not a heavy read. What I find in most books on investments and corporate finance is that it is too prescriptive with the technical "how-to"s. Voluminous texts on decision-making methods and technical specifics on how to deal with various business processes and functions often confuse and sometimes, discourage corporate newcomers and young apprentices. Without knowing where to start, it can be a truly frustrating and stressful experience. The ramifications of not starting off under the right guidance can be disastrous, because one's wisdom does not grow with age or with the wrong kind of experience.

"A wealth of information often leads to a dearth of attention" and in the seeming chaos in the world of business and investments, forming a view is more and more difficult,

especially if we wishes to form one that underscores clarity and foresight. As Lord Petyr Baelish aka Littlefinger from the cult series, Game of Thrones, once said, *"Chaos is not a pit, Chaos is a ladder"*. Navigating uncertainties is becoming one of the most sought-after traits and skills for modern day knowledge operators. I aim to write a book where the reader can finish in one sitting, because I am quite familiar with the reading habits and level of patience of my target audience, the typical corporate professional.

In this book, I will use the context of forming a view on a company or investment opportunity as an example of how to form a view with clarity and how various actions contribute to the level of conviction of this view. My goal is to assuage anyone coming into the business and investments world, that amid the deluge of information and expectations, there is a way out. And you are already taking the initiative to find that way. I believe that if you begin to internalize these 2 ideas, you will begin to see things in a new light, and thus, be able to pick up new knowledge and develop new insights more efficiently and effectively. This is analogous to the red pill from the science-fiction movie, The Matrix in 1999. In the movie, the main character, Neo is offered the choice to consume between a red pill and a blue pill. The blue pill would allow him to remain in the fabricated reality of the Matrix which is controlled by the Machines. The red pill would lead to his escape from the Matrix and see things as they truly are. You, the reader, are Neo, and you are now offered the same choice.

The first step towards the rest of your life begins with the selection of a good pair of shoes.

It is my aim that these 2 ideas that I am sharing represent this pair of shoes that I am gifting you, as you embark on your journey towards success.

2 THE FIRST IDEA

"Speed is of the essence in the business world."

~Business Adage

This is almost an understatement, if not, a typical platitude we hear at work all the time. Making decisions on the go is not just a desirable attribute but almost a pre-requisite to survive in the corporate jungle. Of course, making good decisions is a different matter altogether, which we will explore later on in this book. Far too often, I have seen how a corporate greenhorn gets paralyzed when he/she is asked to form a view about something within a short period of time. In fact, this is usually the first test of whether a person is going to thrive in a corporate environment or not. So, I have always wondered why is it that some people can form views promptly while some don't. I have heard some personality experts claiming that this can be explained simply by a difference between extroverts and introverts, and the degree of articulation and public speaking training the subjects have had. I used to buy that school of thought, until I found out that many people who are known extroverts also got frozen on the spot, when suddenly asked to form views of their own. One would wonder why. Effective managers seem to be able to organize themselves, and structure processes and initiate tasks to achieve desired objectives promptly. The question, again is why? And How? Some folks will attribute it to experience, which is undeniably important in the corporate context, but when you examine the root cause, it boils down to one important thing. And that is the first idea I like to share with you.

FRAMEWORKS

I cannot stress enough, the importance of frameworks. We form views and make decisions based on certain frameworks that we have formulated since our formative age. One might not have noticed this, but we form views and make decisions all the time. From the moment we wake up, our decision to go to the bathroom, or to brush our teeth all require decision making. Even though these sort of decision-making does not take up much efforts, the preamble to such actions is nonetheless, a result of a mental framework which we have developed since birth. Different people call it differently, some will call this mere habits, others may call them sub-conscious decisions.

Psychologists or cognitive scientists refer this sort of mental frameworks as schemata, which is a fancy word to describe organized thoughts or behaviors. In essence, a schema is a mental framework representing some aspect of what we experience and sense in the world. It is how we experience our life and existence. We have that unique ability to develop schemata when we were young, but as we grow older, we are taught so many different things, and governed by the boundaries and limits set by societal and moral authorities, we begin to develop less and less of such mental frameworks. I have read before in a speed-reading book by Tony Buzan, that as children, our intuition is to use our fingers to point at the words, thus allowing our eyes to "read" the words, but as we began formal education in school and we were taught how to vocalize the words and what those words meant, we began to lose the ability to "read" with our eyes, but in essence, "sub-vocalizing" them to register them in our brain, thus dramatically reducing our ability to speed-read.

I am not a psychologist by training, nor am I an expert in the field of cognitive science, but I will argue that the

The History of Schemata

A British psychologist named Frederic Bartlett first introduced the use of schemata, otherwise known as schemas, as a basic concept as part of his learning theory in the early 20th century. Barlett's theory suggested that our understanding of the world is formed by a network of abstract mental structures.

Theorist Jean Piaget also introduced the term schema and popularized its use through his extensive work in developmental psychology throughout the mid-20th century. According to his stage theory of cognitive development, a child goes through a series of stages of intellectual growth. A schema is both the category of knowledge and the process of acquiring that knowledge. As experiences occur and new information is presented, new schemas are developed and old schemas are changed or modified.

same goes for our ability to form schemata or mental frameworks as we grow older. As we are told about the various rules that we need to abide by and the societal norms that govern our collective behaviors, our brains begin to adopt a relatively indolent approach, one that focuses on receiving information, as opposed to one that focuses on processing those information.

All through our schooling years, we are taught various frameworks in different disciplines. Advancement in learning technologies has also highlighted the importance of project-based learning, with the primary objective to put in practice, the various frameworks that were taught, on how to apply knowledge and manage information. The attention on the realms of creativity and innovation over the last decade has indeed underscored the importance of developing an active brain which processes information effectively. In fact, one of the key roles of academia, aside from imparting knowledge and research, is to develop new and better frameworks to understand the world around us. As access to information becomes easier and easier for more and more people, the future belongs only to those who can best utilize the information to form views and make informed decisions.

A renewed interest in frameworks is thus warranted. Only through good frameworks can we seek to make better sense of the world. Successful people often have good mental frameworks to organize information. Their frameworks are flexible and continuously evolving. They are always keen and willing to refine them. Irrational and dogmatic frameworks are seldom the answer to growth and development of wisdom.

One common trait among highly effective and successful people is their use of frameworks. However, you may ask, we all went to the same schools, we learnt the same stuff, what makes them so special? Well, here is where it makes all the difference. Highly effective and successful people are able to mentally-categorize the various known frameworks they like or choose, and deploy them at will to different situations. This is a large part of their secret to success.

These are people who can form views effectively largely because of their ability to develop and deploy mental frameworks in their area of work. However, the masters and investment sages took this ability to the next level by developing what I refer to as Helicopter-Frameworks. Before I describe what helicopter-frameworks are, allow me to explain the concept of helicopter view.

Helicopter View

Helicopter view is a concept that was made popular by the Royal Dutch Shell Company since the 1970s, after an internal study that identifies a common characteristic of its highly successful executives. These individuals were equipped with the ability to "zoom in" and "zoom out" a situation, and scale the ladder of abstraction up and down with ease. What this means is that they are able to think strategically how each operational adjustment impacts the entire organization and process, and how does it contribute to the mission of the company. The metaphorical representation of a helicopter is the ability to rise from one spot up and down to see "the big picture".

In the early 20th century where assembly-line industrialization introduced by Henry Ford[4], transformed modern commerce, there is a large focus on task-oriented processes, to ensure seamless operations. However, the

---

[4] Henry Ford was the icon for assembly-line industrialization at that time. Division of labor being one of the hallmarks of capitalism, contributes substantially to increased efficiency in production and was manifested greatly in Henry Ford's automobile factories.

post-WWII era is marked by rapid globalization and managers with the ability to see the "big picture" and integrate complex links are highly prized. Seeing patterns in a tapestry of chaos allows them to pin-point opportunities to capitalize. As such, this trait becomes very important in leadership development. In fact, many well-known companies like GE, IBM, Hewlett Packard and the Japanese multinational companies began to popularize the importance of "Helicopter View" by embedding this skill to be assessed in their respective performance management processes. To facilitate the development of this skill, role or job rotation within large companies becomes a typical leadership development practice. This allows managers and executives to understand the roles and functions, and in so doing, allows them to provide fresh perspectives on how to integrate various disparate processes and strengthen the institution accordingly.

In the realm of investing, the helicopter view is a crucial skill. Investment sages that I have seen or worked with, displayed this ability to have a helicopter view. However, this is not just about seeing the "big picture". Any investment professionals will tell u that there are many elements to the investment process, and the need to be meticulous and scrutinize the minute details is equally important in any due-diligence or valuation-modeling exercises. Having a helicopter view means just that, the ability to "zoom in and out" at will. Making sense of a situation amid chaos and multiple data-points, is what you call "Forming a View".

"Not seeing the wood for the trees"

The tendency to get lost in the details is the prime reason for analysis paralysis, and it happens more often than we think. Only by anchoring one's thought process with an all-encompassing purpose or objective can we conjure the sustainable energy to focus on the tasks at hand. This is where "Helicopter-frameworks" come into the picture.

Helicopter-frameworks are a sort of master frameworks which are dynamic in nature. Highly effective and successful people used them and continuously refine them to suit different situations. You can think of helicopter-frameworks like that of a Lego-brick structure, one that can be modified at different areas where necessary. Most well-known global consultants such as McKinsey and Co or the Boston Consulting Group have developed similar master frameworks and institutionalize them to embed them into all their associates and partners.

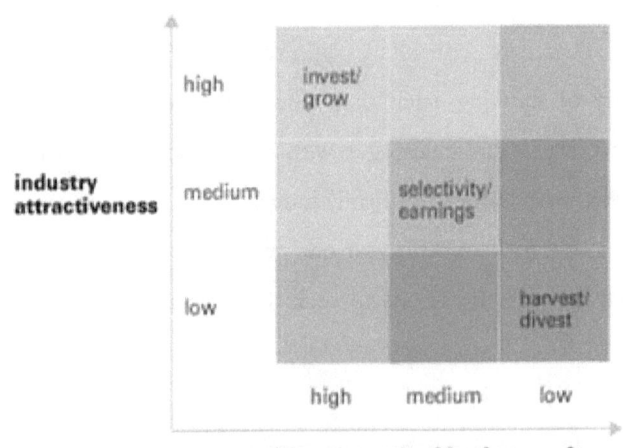

Fig 1. The Classic 70s GE-McKinsey 9 Box Matrix

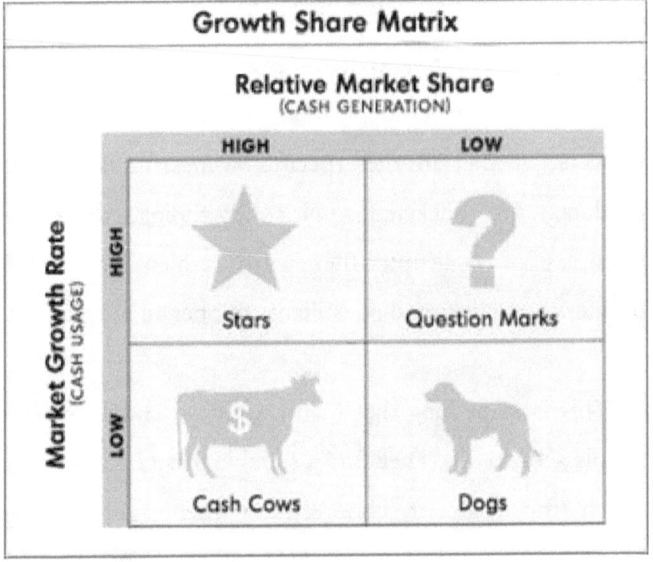

Fig 2. The Classic BCG Growth-Share Matrix

Therefore, consultants are "equipped" with the right way of thinking, such that they can approach any issues and intellectual challenges with confidence. With such a helicopter-framework firmly internalized, these consultants are able to "zoom in and out" whenever they desire and ask the right questions to seek the information they need in order to form a view.

The aforementioned charts show 2 classic frameworks which many business school students have learnt and used, but any corporate veteran will tell you that those are very simplified frameworks, and explaining what each boxes or quadrants mean is not going to get anyone impressed. The challenge is not to describe what they mean, but how the subjects (whether are they specific business units/lines or products) are bucketed. Notwithstanding, these are examples of Helicopter-frameworks which enable the business executives and consultants to operate effectively.

This is something that highly effective and successful people seek to do. They find a suitable master-framework, which they like or choose, and then keep drilling themselves to use them in different scenarios, refining them along the way, as they accrue experience. In this way, their time will not be wasted, as every single moment spent at work or in life, they are strengthening the foundation of their mental frameworks. This is their secret to feeling enriched with their experiences.

Helicopter-frameworks help to compartmentalize various issues and facilitate decision-making process, because at the end of all brainstorming and discussions, the decision is all that matters. Forming views constitute options for leaders to decide. In the world of investments, a decision to invest or divest is the goal in discussions. There are always various perspectives, which can be the result of different mental-frameworks in action. Those are generally acceptable and well-appreciated among professionals, but the only unacceptable one, in any respectable institution is an illogical, irrational decision, which is usually one that is made without any frameworks.

3 AN EXAMPLE OF A HELICOPTER FRAMEWORK

The first word in "Analyst" is "Anal"

~ Barton Biggs, Diary of a Hedgehog

Being a good analyst is the first step towards becoming a good investor. What I have observed for many business and investment greenhorns is their tendency to get lost in the ocean of information and details, that they forget the most important objective of all - the view of the subject company in question. Reading through annual reports and analysts reports of a subject company without a clear objective is the sure path towards confusion, stress and frustration.

Following the previous chapter on frameworks, I will

like to introduce a traditional one used by many sophisticated investment professionals to form a view about a company. Using this example of a Helicopter-framework, you will be able to see how an analyst can function effectively, and avoid getting lost in the details. Such a framework guides the analyst to seek out the necessary information he/she needs such that they accrue to the satisfactory level of conviction in the view to be formed.

In Joel Greenblatt's classic 2005 book, the "Little Book that Beats the Market", he shared a "Magic Formula" for individual investors to adopt. In fact, he back-tested the formula with stock price data across various time horizons, and highlighted its outperformance over several market benchmarks. It is truly remarkable that this "magic formula" is able to consistently deliver outstanding returns, but any circumspect analyst will begin to question whether is it applicable to institutional investors or relevant to their work. That is a fair question. Before we address that question, let us scrutinize what this magic formula is. According to Joel, this magic formula comprises of two main factors: Return on Capital and Earnings Yield. Over a one year holding period, the companies or stock with the highest Return on Capital and Earnings Yield will most likely deliver outperformance relative to the rest of the market constituents.

Let us drill deeper into the two main factors, starting with Return on Capital (RoC). What is Return on Capital? Return on capital is a ratio that indicates the efficiency and profitability of a company's capital investments. Why is this important to investors? Very simply, companies that are competent in generating profits from their operations tend to have competitive advantages or what some business people refer to as "Economic Moats", and such advantages usually translate into superior investment returns.

RoC provides a good example of a Helicopter-framework which allows the user to drill-in and zoom out at will. In Joel Greenblatt's book, he defined it as

EBIT/(Net Working Capital + Net Fixed Assets)
i.e. the ratio of pre-tax operating earnings (EBIT) to tangible capital employed (Net Working Capital + Net Fixed Assets).

There are several variances to this formula, such as ROCE or Return on Capital Employed which is calculated as EBIT/(Total Assets - Current Liabilities). Some analysts use NOPAT or (Net Operating Profit after Tax) over the book value of Invested Capital which refers to the summation of the Net Debt and Equity. However, the idea is more or less the same. A good proxy that good analysts and investors use to form quick views is the Return on Equity or Return on Assets ratio. However, knowing when to use which ratio or proxy depends very much what perspective or lens is one wearing. It is an example of how this Helicopter-framework is dynamic and can be constantly refined, but for simplicity sake, I will use Return on Equity (RoE) to illustrate how to do so for a typical operating company, where the analyst is assessing the company's operating performance from the perspective of a stockholder/equity holder.

Sophisticated institutional investors have often looked at RoE with keen interest, and any good analysis on a company's operating performance will include a deep scrutiny on the key components of RoE. The RoE number is a good measure of how the company creates value, but it tells a lot more than that, if we decompose it further. This practice is first initiated by the Dupont Corporation all the way back in the 1920s. The DuPont Corporation is an American chemicals company established since the early 19th century. It has a rich history and is a fixture within the Dow Jones Industrial Index since the early 1930s. DuPont played a large part in the industrialization of US and shaped our modern way of life by developing many useful polymers, with notable examples such as Nylon and Teflon. As the company grew larger, the DuPont leadership in the 1920s decided that the best way to identify areas to unlock value is to find out the key drivers of each business line. This was probably one of the earliest accounts of how a helicopter-framework was used to assist the formation of management views and decisions.

Given that the first known management consultancy firm was established by Arthur D Little, a MIT Professor back in 1886, I often wondered whether a similar form of analysis to the Dupont-formula began since the roots of management consulting history.

History of Management Consulting

Arthur D. Little, a MIT professor started the first management consultancy firm way back in 1886. It was subsequently incorporated in 1909, following the growing interest in "Management" in the higher-education curriculum. Another notable early management consulting firm, Booz Allen Hamilton[5], was also founded in 1914, as corporations become more prevalent in the United States of America. Edwin G. Booz, the founder was a graduate of the Kellogg School of Management at Northwestern University, and the firm served mostly government and large corporate clients, who were primarily the wealthy and known capitalists of the early 20th century. In 1926, James O. McKinsey, a professor of Managerial Accounting at the University of Chicago, Booth School of Business, founded the now globally-known McKinsey & Co. AT Kearney was also founded around the same time in 1926 in Chicago, Illinois.

---

[5] Booz Allen Hamilton has transformed from a management consulting firm into one that focuses on the provision of management, technology and security services, primarily to civilian government agencies and as a security and defense contractor to defense and intelligence agencies, as well as civil and commercial services

The recession of 1913-1914 led to a significant drop in gross domestic production and wage levels, and during this period, the Federal Reserve Act was signed into law by President Woodrow Wilson, thereby establishing the Federal Reserve System. As with today's case with the Dodd Frank Act of 2010, the establishment of the Federal Reserve System was a major game-changer for businesses, but not many people understood the impact of it. Management consulting saw its roots since those days, as the demand for sound professional advice grew. The Glass-Steagall Banking Act of the 1930s and post-war consolidation and growth saw the increasing focus on Strategy, Management and Organization, and consulting work became more and more appreciated within the business community. Together with the well-known business schools such as Harvard Business School and the University of Chicago Booth School of Business, various tools and methodologies were developed in the 1960s and 1970s and institutionalized within the well-known consulting firms. New firms such as Boston Consulting Group (BCG) were founded in the 1970s by Bruce D Henderson, a Harvard Business School alumnus. Bill Bain, and a group of about 6 other partners and managers from BCG later left to start a new consulting firm, Bain &

Co in 1973, focusing on longer-horizon assignments.

The early 1980s also saw the advent of Private Equity Buyout firms. In 1984, Bill Bain formed Bain Capital, a private equity firm, because the leading management consultants believed that they can indeed deploy their proprietary capital to invest in companies where their value-creation plans can truly unlock or create value. An interesting point to note is that Mitt Romney, a 2012 US Republican Presidential Candidate, who was also a Bain & Co partner at that time, was named its CEO then. With the exponential increase in credit since the 1980s, and a flush of capital, leveraged buyouts became more and more common. With the infamous US$31bn takeover of RJR Nabisco by Kohlberg Kravis Roberts in 1989 (Readers may wish to read up more on this from the popular book entitled "Barbarians at the Gate"; A movie of the same name, directed by Glenn Jordan, was also released in the early 1990s) that marked the high-point of private equity and events leading to the savings and loans crisis in the late 80s and early 90s, management consulting took a hit. However, the introduction of the World Wide Web and prevalence of information technology saw a revival of consulting services, which are more skewed towards the IT consulting segment. However, global management consultants are facing competitive pressure from global accounting firms such as PricewaterhouseCoopers, KPMG, Ernst & Young, and Deloitte Touche.

Scale and the institutionalization of knowledge base from previous clients' projects which span geographies and markets become crucial in this industry and helicopter-frameworks become more and more relevant in today's context than ever, as they help to synthesize insights and deliver fresh perspectives in an effective manner.

With the implicit endorsement of a world-class institution, the DuPont Formula thus gained global recognition and was eventually adopted by sophisticated investors and business analysts. Now, let's look more closely at what the DuPont formula is about.

In its most basic form, the return on equity is calculated as follows:

$$Return\ on\ Equity\ (ROE)$$
$$= \frac{Net\ Income}{Average\ Shareholder'sEquity}$$

And average shareholder's equity refers to the average

of this year's and previous year's balance sheet shareholder equity figures. Shareholders' equity is also called book value, which is the difference between total assets and total liabilities, or sometimes refer to as Net Asset Value.

The higher a company's ROE, the better the management of the company is at utilizing the investors' capital to generate profits.

Yet, one will be fooled to look at the ROE figures at such a simplistic way, because there are risks associated with high returns. A good investor or analyst will tell you that we cannot isolate risk from returns. The Tao[6] of Investment Enlightenment is that "Return" is the "Yang", and "Risk" is the "Yin" and both goes hand-in-hand. Let me explain further: A company needs capital to grow its business but it cannot grow earnings faster than its current ROE without raising new capital. Companies do that by either selling new shares via a process known as Rights Issue, borrow money from banks or by issuing debt

---

[6] Tao, is an oriental concept from Tao-teching, written by the ancient Chinese philosopher, Lao Tzu. A subset of Tao, which is originally derived from I-Ching (The Book of Changes), is the concept of "yin and yang", which is used to describe how seemingly opposite or contrary forces are interconnected and interdependent in the natural world

securities to fixed income investors. In essence, the ROE serves like a speed limit on a firm's growth rate, and it is actually a good way to sanity-check any assumptions on a firm's future prospects using this rule. However, there are costs involved for both such activities: Borrowing from banks or issuing debt securities leads to higher interest expense, which can lower net income; and selling more shares dilute existing shareholders' claim to the net income, as dividends need to be paid out to a larger number of shareholders. All these increases the risk corresponding to said investment.

However, this formula can be further decomposed into the following:

Return on Equity (ROE)

$$= \frac{Net\ Income}{Average\ Shareholder's Equity}$$

$$= \frac{Net\ Income}{Sales\ Revenue} (Net\ Profit\ Margin) \times$$

$$\frac{Sales\ Revenue}{Average\ Total\ Assets} (Asset\ Turnover) \times$$

$$\frac{Average\ Total\ Assets}{Average\ Shareholder's\ Equity} (Equity\ Multiplier)$$

Therefore, simply put, ROE = Net profit margin ×
asset turnover × equity multiplier. Using this formula, the
reader can now zoom in this helicopter framework to drill
deeper into each components to see where this company is
doing right ... or wrong.

Net Profit Margin

Net profit margin, or Net margin for short, is one of the
most important figures in finance. It can be further
broken down into operating income margin and gross
margin. Essentially, it illustrates how much profit can be
made from every unit of sales made. Net profit margin is a
function of several things, but the key one is the price of
the company's product resulting from the competitive
nature of the industry. Ceteris paribus[7], if there is no
competitive pressure in a particular industry, a company
can technically have immense pricing power. Famous
capitalists of the early 20th century, such as John D
Rockefeller and Andrew Carnegie used to own monopolies
in the oil and steel industry and enjoyed high profit
margins as a result. These days, given anti-trust regulations
and higher competition, companies or industries with high
net margins are no longer common. That is the reason

---

[7] Ceteris Paribus means assuming everything else being equal

why innovation in companies is so important in today's context, because it is the only way where a celebrated companies today can continuously maintain high profit margins. Companies pursue research and development for the purpose of innovating new products and services and bring them to market. At the early stage of a product life-cycle, companies are able to secure higher prices for such product and services but as they progress through the life-cycle, new market entrants come in to eat a slice of the pie. Very soon, a blue ocean[8] will transform into a red ocean through sheer competitive forces from the new entrants, therefore chipping away the high net margins.

It should be noted that there are several good frameworks to analyze pricing power and competitive forces. Dr Philip Kotler's 4P framework and Professor Michael Porter's 5 Forces framework are good places to start, but in the spirit of brevity and focus, I will not be covering them. I do, however, hope that the reader can appreciate how this helicopter-framework known as DuPont formula is able to open a new door for people to form views and insights. Each level of analysis is meant to

---

[8] Blue ocean refers to uncontested market segment, as detailed in the 2005 book "Blue Ocean Strategy" by W. Chan Kim and Renée Mauborgne

lend further credence and conviction to the ultimate view.

Asset Turnover

The asset turnover ratio is the ratio of a company's sales to its assets. It is essentially an efficiency ratio which illustrates how well the company is using its assets to generate sales revenue.

There are also a number of variants of the ratio such as fixed asset turnover ratio and working capital turnover ratio, where the variable is the denominator which can be average fixed assets or average working capital respectively. This depends entirely on the industry or company in question, as some industries are capital-intensive, and low asset turnover is normal, given the large value of fixed assets.

$$Total\ Asset\ Turnover = \frac{Net\ Sales}{Average\ Total\ Assets}$$

$$Fixed\ Asset\ Turnover = \frac{Net\ Sales}{Average\ Fixed\ Assets}$$

$$Working\ Capital\ Turnover = \frac{Net\ Sales}{Average\ Net\ Working\ Capital}$$

In essence, if a company can generate more sales with fewer assets, then it has a higher turnover ratio. A lower turnover ratio highlights that the said company may not be using its assets optimally. However, a good analyst or investor will not see this in isolation. The asset turnover ratio can be a reflection of the pricing strategy as well as companies with lower profit margins tend to have higher asset turnover ratios and vice-versa.

Therefore, the next level of a good analysis via due-diligence will be to explore the pricing strategy, and assess the level of inventory management and the execution capabilities of the sales team. From there, a lot of detailed views can then be formed, such as areas of improvements for supply chain management or other potential value-creation opportunities with respect to branding and advertising.

This is what the due-diligence process is all about. Many corporate greenhorns especially in the investment world do not know how to conduct a proper due-diligence. In fact, many so-called corporate "veterans" are also guilty as charged. They may go into a management meeting, going through a list of standard prepared questions, but not knowing what is the end goal in mind. It is more common than one can imagine. This is also the main reason why we hear many horror stories of mergers and acquisitions gone awry over the years, and the worst part is that companies do not learn from such mistakes because they are not even sure where they have gone wrong. Having a helicopter-framework thus helps analysts or investors to ensure that the end goal is kept in the cross-hair at all time, and more importantly, should there be any mistakes or lapse of judgment, they are able to pinpoint where in the due-diligence or analysis process that they can rectify. Any young apprentices in the business will do well to heed this advice.

Equity Multiplier

The equity multiplier is the factor that highlights the risk associated with the return. It is defined as a measure of financial leverage and is a method of evaluating a company's ability to use its debt for financing its assets. The equity multiplier is also sometimes referred to as the leverage ratio or the financial leverage ratio. A higher equity multiplier indicates higher financial leverage, which consequently, means the company is relying more on debt to finance its assets.

Calculated by dividing average total assets by the average stockholder's equity, some people also used an alternate formula as follows:

$$\text{Equity Multiplier} = \frac{1}{Equity\ Ratio}$$

where Equity Ratio refers to the ratio of the average total shareholder's equity to the average total assets.

Therefore, as you can infer, a company can technically boost its return on equity by increasing its equity multiplier. What this means is the increase of borrowings or debt, and therefore elevates the risk associated with the company.

Always remembering that equity or stockholders are always subordinated to the Debt Holders, the higher the equity multiplier simply means there are more stakeholders who have a higher priority of payment than the equity holders during times of liquidation.

Fig 3: A typical Corporate Capital Structure

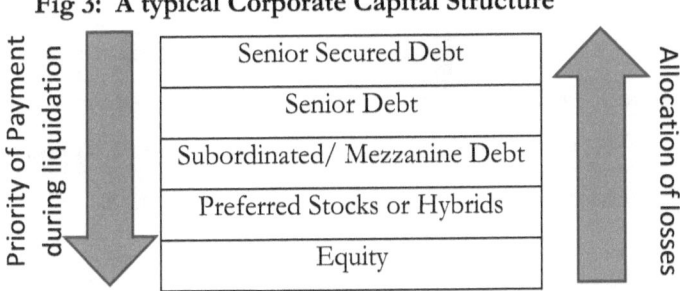

There are various ways of analyzing the capital structure, but as I have repeatedly mentioned, this is not a book to teach you all the concepts in the realm of corporate finance, but a book to show you the importance of helicopter frameworks.

Debt management is an important part of any company's operations. The equity multiplier is actually the introducing variable to assessing the competencies of the Finance department, under the leadership of the Chief Financial Officer or CFO. From this equity multiplier, analysts and investors can then drill down to explore different areas of how a company manages its asset and liability duration, as well as ensuring that the operating cash-flows are sufficient to cover the interest expenses.

Any stress points are usually exposed through such a leverage analysis, which is typical of any good due diligence process. In the world of investments, identifying a good company is simply not good enough, what it takes is to identify when will it be a good time to make an approach to make an investment, and the answer usually starts in the analysis of the equity multiplier, and consequently, the leverage and cash-flow management.

One must always remember that if a company is well-managed, and if the industry which it is in is fabulous, there is often no reason why the company will look to raise new capital for a discounted value, but if a good analyst or investor can identify stress points, they will be able to make a timely offer, which will be particularly rewarding in the future.

There are many reasons why a company raised equity or debt. Sometimes, it may be puzzling at first. For example, Apple Inc raised US$17bn of bond debt in 2Q 2013 to pay dividends to its shareholders, when it had more than US$140bn in cash on its balance sheet. However, upon deeper scrutiny, one is able to understand further. In this case, it has a lot to do with tax burden due to many of Apple's offshore operations, primarily in Asia, and this large bond issue is considered a smart move[9] by institutional investors worldwide.

Let us see how to put that all together in an example. Assuming a Food & Beverages company, Company ABC has the following financials in the Financial Year (T).

Net Income = USD 8.5 billion

Total Revenue = USD 50 billion

Average Total Assets = USD80 billion

Average Shareholders' Equity = USD30 billion

As we can see, the Return on Equity (RoE) is simply = 8.5 *10^9/30 *10^9 = **28.3%**

By plugging the numbers into the formulas laid out earlier in this chapter, we can easily break the RoE down further into:

Return on Equity (ROE)

$$= \frac{Net\ Income}{Average\ Shareholder'sEquity}$$

---

[9] Source:
http://www.moneynews.com/InvestingAnalysis/Schwarzman-Apple-bonds-housing/2013/05/02/id/502419

$$= \frac{Net\ Income}{Sales\ Revenue}\ (Net\ Profit\ Margin)\ \times$$

$$\frac{Sales\ Revenue}{Average\ Total\ Assets}\ (Asset\ Turnover)\ \times$$

$$\frac{Average\ Total\ Assets}{Average\ Shareholder's\ Equity}\ (Equity\ Multiplier)$$

And since

Net Income Margin = 8.5 *10^9/50 *10^9 = **17.0%**

Asset Turnover = 50 *10^9/80 *10^9 = **62.5%**

Equity Multiplier = 80 *10^9/30 *10^9 = **2.67x/(267%)**

Return on Equity (RoE) =

17.0% x 62.5% x 2.67x = 28.3%

So now, as you can see, a simple Helicopter-framework like the DuPont Formula is able to help align an analyst or investor's focus to form fresh new and useful views and insights. There is no more fear, as every step of the analysis is contributing to an ultimate view of this company – what constitutes to the return of equity to the company.

What I have shown is a simple 3-step DuPont formula, there are some other variances to this, notably the 5-step DuPont formula which is equally powerful, and we can get an overview of it in the appendix of this book.

4 THE SECOND IDEA

"When you sit on a hot stove for two minutes, it feels like two hours. But, when you sit with a nice girl for two hours, it feels like two minutes. That's relativity!"

~ Albert Einstein, Relativity:
The Special and the General Theory

In the last couple of chapters, I have expounded the importance of employing helicopter-frameworks to drill down various levels of a particular subject in order to form a view. I have also used a classic example known as the DuPont analysis to show you how to form a view about a company's operating performance. However, as I have described in the introduction, the use of frameworks, being the First Idea, is merely one side of the pair of shoes that I seek to equip you on your journey towards business and investment success. There is another shoe that is of equal importance as well, and that is the second idea I like to share with you:

RELATIVITY

When people talk or think about relativity, the formula $E = mc^2$ so famously proposed by Albert Einstein in 1905 comes into mind. This is also the equation that ignited the infamous Manhattan project, leading to the nuclear age. Quite frankly, without this equation or the suggestion that a small amount of matter can generate a large amount of energy, I really doubt anyone would have conceived the idea of building the atomic bomb. Therefore, the idea of relativity can be quite intimidating to many people.

Yet, the concept of relativity in our context here is rather simple. I am simply using this as a fancy synonym to "comparison". The Art of Comparing is an especial skill in the business and investment world. Business schools also emphasized the importance of benchmarking, which is the process of comparing one's business processes and operating performance metrics to peers, typically in the same industry. Investment analysis is almost always about identifying the right comparable group/set. In fact, if someone brings you an investment opportunity, and only focuses on everything great about the company, but mentions nothing about its competitors, or how it performed operationally relative to its peers or comparable group, then it is typically a red-flag.

Furthermore, the concept of relativity expands beyond just comparing a company's metrics with its peers. It also refers to the comparison of its current metrics with historical performance metrics.

Lightning doesn't strike the same 'spot' twice, but it sure does hit the same area in pretty much the same way

As mentioned in the previous chapter, we can decompose the Return on Equity into its various components and identify which are the primary drivers of performance, but we will not be able to know how it fares compared to its peers, and we won't know how it fares compared to its own history. The helicopter-framework such as DuPont analysis can only provide a snapshot of a company, but true insight can only be generated when this snapshot is juxtaposed with other snapshots. For example, if a company's RoE is high or above 20%, and it seems very attractive, it could turn up to be a bad investment if its industry peers are showing RoEs of more than 30%. Also, the investor or analyst will not know whether this subject company's RoE has declined or improved over the previous years. An investor is often considering an investment in a company for its future prospects, and if the trend indicates a declining RoE, it certainly does not lend any new level of confidence to justify a higher valuation. Therefore, it is crucial to juxtapose a snapshot with various dimensions. Of course, I am not suggesting that history will always repeat in exactly the same way, but any good investor knows that the human fallacy to forget and repeat similar mistakes is extremely high.

A good investor and analyst has to develop this "Relativity" mindset. Several frameworks from major consulting houses are developed with the primary objective to allow management to visualize this "Relativity" with ease, using different matrices. Such frameworks either compare the different business units, product lines or country operations, but the goal is the same – to compare one another through a certain pair of lens. The most effective management executives know which pair of lens to use, and often enough, this is the first step towards conceptualizing a sound business and value creation plan. This is simply because, identifying and scrutinizing why and how a subject entity, whether is it a company, individual or business unit is doing better than the rest can throw light into the development of best practices as well. Comparing with its historical performance can also help determine whether a certain change to existing processes and management is bearing fruit. Furthermore, comparing across different years and business cycles can throw even more insight into what to expect in the near future.

Following the example in the previous chapter, I will now show you how comparing across different years can allow the analyst or investor to sharpen his/her focus and ask the right questions. If you recall our example, a Food & Beverages company, Company ABC has a RoE of 28.3% in Financial Year (T), which is pretty good even on a standalone basis. When we decompose the RoE further, we found out that its:

Net Income Margin = 8.5 *10^9/50 *10^9 = **17.0%**
Asset Turnover = 50 *10^9/80 *10^9 = **62.5%**
Equity Multiplier = 80 *10^9/30 *10^9 = **2.67x/(267%)**

Not bad, we are getting more information, but this still does not tell us much about this company. Let's look deeper, and explore its historical financials.

Company ABC

In USD'000s	FY T	FY T-1	FYT-2
ROE	28.3%	44.4%	28.6%
Revenue	50,000	40,000	30,000
Net Income	8,500	12,000	7,000
Ave Total Assets	80,000	64,000	47,500
Ave Shr Equity	30,000	27,000	24,500

We can see in the above table that while Company ABC's RoE of 28.3% in financial year T is pretty good, it is a sharp drop from the previous financial year T-1, where its RoE is 44.4%, and a good analyst or investor would do well to understand why and the DuPont analysis applied across the years will provide a good point to begin.

Company ABC

In USD'000s	FY T	FY T-1	FYT-2
ROE	28.3%	44.4%	28.6%
Revenue	50,000	40,000	30,000
Net Income	8,500	12,000	7,000
Ave Total Assets	80,000	64,000	47,500
Ave Shr Equity	30,000	27,000	24,500
Net Margin	17.0%	30.0%	23.3%
Asset Turnover	62.5%	62.5%	63.2%
Equity Multiplier	266.7%	237.0%	193.9%

We can thus see that for Company ABC, while the asset turnover, which measures the operational efficiency of the firm, has remained pretty much constant over the 3 years, there is a substantial drop in the margins and a notable increase in the equity multiplier.

As with any good helicopter frameworks, this allows the analyst and investor to ask the "Right" questions, such as:

- What constitutes the drop in Net Margin?
- Was it due to a drop in pricing power?

- o Was this caused by increasing competition?
- o Were new products introduced by the company able to command similar profit margins or less?
- o Was it a structural development for the industry?
- o How is the management going to address this issue?
- o Could it be that FY T-1 was an anomaly year, and if so, what constituted the bumper year?
- o What is the management currently doing to ensure that its margins remain high?
- Why has the company's asset turnover being constant?
    - o Could it has better exploit its growing size and enjoy bigger economies of scales?
    - o What is the management's plan to improve its asset turnover going forward?
- Was it mainly due to the increase in leverage?
    - o Is the company paying too much in debt?
    - o Is the company's cost of debt too high?
    - o Is the company able to cope with this increase in leverage?

As you can see, a simple exercise using such a helicopter framework applied across a few years, can elicit a lot more insight for the analyst or investor. The most important thing is that all the answers that one received will be able to lend conviction to the forecast that the analyst is making. No longer will it be a mere "stabbing-in-the-dark" but there will be a clear basis for the view formed.

In fact, most private equity firms go a few steps beyond performing such analysis. Other than merely assessing management capabilities to execute on any value-creation plans, to boost the margins, asset turnover or equity multiplier, they built a pool of operational capabilities through their own network, and execute them, should the existing management fail to perform. This will ensure a more proactive stance towards translating "numbers-on-a-paper" into actual value created. Firms like Bain, Carlyle and TPG built very huge and successful empires doing precisely that, and in so doing, they have helped to transform industries in the US and globally, especially in the last couple of decades.

At this point, I would like to share with you another

movie experience. As you can tell, I am sort of a movie buff, and I do sincerely believe that movies are good extensions to the development of one's imagination, which as I will expound in later chapters, is an important skill and trait to have in order to become a successful investor or leader. Developing one's imagination allows one to derive various scenarios which will pan out, helping the decision-maker to form good views.

In the 2013 fairy-tale adapted movie, Jack the Giant-Slayer starring Nicholas Hoult, Stanley Tucci and Ewan McGregor, I remembered a scene where the proud king and his captain proclaimed that the Gates to the City are the strongest and tallest ever built, and it will withstand any onslaught or attacks from any adversaries. In the end, these walls proved puny and almost no resistance to the attacking Giants. So what was the message in all this? What cardinal mistake did the king or the captain make? The answer is obvious on hindsight – While they may have built the strongest castle walls and gates to match any foes they know of in the past, they miscalculated and severely underestimated their adversaries this time round – the Giants!

Therefore, despite using a helicopter-framework,

comparing a company just against its past performance is similar to just building a castle wall based on past experiences. We need to also compare the company against other companies, in order to gain further insights, form better views on what actions to undertake. Let us use our favorite F&B company once more, Company ABC, but to illustrate how to perform a peer comparison we must introduce its arch-rival, Company XYZ.

Company XYZ

In USD'000s	FY T	FY T-1	FYT-2
ROE	30.2%	30.8%	40. 0%
Revenue	66,500	58,000	43,000
Net Income	6,500	6,000	5,800
Ave Total Assets	70,000	54,000	38,000
Ave Shr Equity	21,500	19,500	14,500

Applying a similar DuPont analysis we find that for Company XYZ,

	FY T	FY T-1	FYT-2
Net Margin	9.8%	10.3%	13.5%
Asset Turnover	95.0%	107.4%	113.2%
Equity Multiplier	325.6%	276.9%	262.1%

So it is very apparent that Company ABC's products command a premium margin over its chief competitor, but it can certainly do better in improving its operational efficiency. However, as we can see from the equity multiplier of both companies, we can see that there is quite a significant difference, and this provide a good place to start for any further work or analysis to be done.

- Is Company ABC underleveraged? Is Company XYZ overleveraged?
- What constitutes such a high asset turnover for Company XYZ, and what can Company ABC replicate to boost its asset turnover values?
- What constitutes such a significant pricing premium that result in the great difference in the Net Margins?
- Are there other products in the Company ABC's Research & Development pipeline that will sustain such a lead over Company XYZ?

Again, I have given you a brief idea of how the combination of deploying a helicopter-framework, and coupled with the power of a "Relativity" mindset, can help to generate more relevant insights and assisting the analyst or investor to form good views.

5 OVERLAYS

Shrek: "For your information, there's a lot more
to ogres than people think."
Donkey: Example?
Shrek: Example... uh... ogres are like onions!
[holds up an onion, which Donkey sniffs]
Donkey: They stink?
Shrek: Yes... No!
Donkey: Oh, they make you cry?
Shrek: No!
Donkey: Oh, you leave 'em out in the sun, they get all brown, start
sproutin' little white hairs...
Shrek: [peels an onion] NO! Layers. Onions have layers. Ogres have
layers. Onions have layers. You get it? We both have layers.

$\sim$ Shrek (2001)

In the previous chapters, I have shared with you how the two ideas — Helicopter-frameworks and Relativity represent the two sides of the pair of shoes which I hoped to equip you with, on your journey towards forming good views in the world of investments and business. However, equipped with this pair of shoes does not equate to immediate success. Equipped with a good pair of shoes is one thing, but the journey ahead is going to be more exciting and enriching if you learn to adopt different "overlays". What are overlays?

In the military, field commanders were often told to establish operation-plans for various missions. There were a multitude of different missions such as search-and-destroy, reconnaissance, supply-sabotage and more. Sometimes, most of such missions are held in the same area, and the same map is used by different military units and divisions. Therefore, maps are often crucial items during a mission. However, in order to coordinate actions between different divisions, from Logistics to Artillery to the Armor divisions and the Infantry, field commanders and strategists use clear PVC (plastic) sheets to lay out whatever plans they have devised on top of the operations map. Other than the obvious reason that drawing out action plan on the same map would utterly disfigure the map beyond recognition, the main objective for using plastic clear sheets over the operations map is such that each unit commander can focus on just his/her respective course of action. And when all the clear sheets are put on top of each other, the unit commanders can all see the "big picture", and how their respective courses of action will contribute to the main mission objective. These clear PVC or plastic sheets where action plans are laid out are known as overlays.

Types of Military Operations

Military operations can be classified by the scale and scope of force deployment, and their impact on the wider conflict. The scope of military operations can be categorized as the following few:

Theater: An operation over a large, and typically covers an entire continent It also represents a strategic national commitment to the conflict with general goals that encompass areas of consideration outside of the military such as the economic and political impacts. For example, in HBO's award-winning epic War Series - Band of Brothers and The Pacific, we saw the detailed and gory depiction of battle scenes in both the Atlantic and the Pacific Theaters of World War II.

Campaign: Typically smaller in scale than a theatre operation, or a more limited geographic and operational strategic commitment, involving a specific region or the size of a city or country, and need not represent total national commitment to a conflict.

Battle: A subset of a campaign that will have specific military goals and geographic objectives. The Battle of

Normandy in 1944 is a classic example of a Battle-scope military operation (codenamed Operation Overlord) involving both Operation Neptune, involving the Normandy landing and Operation Cobra, the inland offensive undertaken by the Allied forces.

Engagement: A tactical combat event or contest for specific area or objective by actions of distinct units.

Strike: A single attack, on a specified target, as a subset of a broader engagement. Strikes have explicit goals, ranging from rendering utility buildings, supply depots or transportation facilities inoperable to assassinations of enemy commanders.

In this post-911 new millennium, where terrorism defines most international and localized conflicts, the rules of engagement have changed significantly. An axiomatic shift from large-scale field operations to smaller-scale urban warfare/FIBUA (Fighting in Build-up Areas) operations to more recently, unmanned drone attacks and cyber-war espionage operations have redefined strategic military planning activities, making them ever more complex, and consequently more strategic and tactical overlays.

Therefore, using the 2 aforementioned ideas will only provide the first basic overlay to form a view of a company or investment opportunity. Corporate veterans and investment analysts will often find them sufficient to form quick views and thus screen investment opportunities with this basic overlay. Under benign operating environment and investment climate (ie a secular bull marker), this is indeed not far from the truth, but under more challenging environments, it is often those investment managers and business leaders who have the ability to develop different sort of overlays that consistently outperform the market and deliver superior returns.

The ability to develop different sort of overlays comes with wisdom and experience. Through the cacophony of noises in the world of business and investments, how do we form differentiated views with clarity? This boils down to what Howard Marks, of Oaktree Capital Management, and author of "The Most Important Thing – Uncommon Sense for the Thoughtful Investor" mentioned – "Second-Level Thinking". Second-level thinking is a way of parsing information that is different from the norm. Second-level thinking requires thoughtful consideration of possible outcomes, probabilities and expectations, as well as understanding how to evaluate the value of a company or investment opportunity relative to all possible scenarios. However, many managers, analysts, and investors are "first-level thinkers" who follow what the mainstream media sensationalizes, and it is not easy to maintain clarity and patience to engage in "second–level" thinking these days. I remembered a notable TV personality once explaining that the 24/7 news cycle was introduced just after the turn of the 21st century, primarily to cover the 911 tragedy – the bombing of the World Trade Center in downtown Manhattan, New York, USA. Ever since then, in order to sustain the very limited universe of news, each news network has to elevate the passion, language and decibel of all sort of news, with key phrases like "Breaking News", "Developing Story", but the aggregate climate and montage is that the world loses its own lexicon, and we no longer know the real meaning behind what's "Urgent" and "Important". As the media sensationalizes the impact of any geopolitical event or natural disaster, it is most common for most people to focus on the immediate impact, but in the heat of "fighting-the-current-fire", they ignore the longer term impact.

For example, after a major hurricane or tornado attack, first-level thinkers may be prone to identify immediate opportunities, by forming negative views about the market, and trade on it. In this case, people who form such views are aplenty, and with the around-the-clock accentuating the messages, it is often a competition of who is faster than the next person in the trade. However, second-level thinkers consider much more than this. As the first-level thinkers struggle to compete in the red-ocean to make the marginal profits from shorting the market, the second-level thinkers consider the future prospect of reconstruction, and which industries or investment opportunities will benefit as a result, which will suffer a structural economic impact as a result etc. Second-level thinkers will thus measure the impact of the damage, and assess when the reconstruction efforts will begin, as they understand that survivors cannot be staying in made shift shelters forever, and demand for construction materials and furniture will surge post such a crisis. Claims for damages on insurance companies will occur, thus creating different sorts of opportunities for different sort of businesses. When one engages in second-level thinking, he/she will uncover a lot more insights and form more useful views than merely competing in the red-ocean of who's-faster. Superior performance can thus be sustained because they can identify clearly what opportunities suit which circumstances.

Another good example is the massive flood in Bangkok, Thailand in 2011. Many first-time thinkers will consider the negative impact of such a flood, and thus short the market or avoid the market entirely, without considering the opportunities. Second-level thinkers will identify that the flood happened in regions where auto-part manufacturers congregate, and would thus cause a major global supply chain shock to the automobile industry. They may also identify that the flood would destroy the rice crops and cause a massive supply shock to rice - a staple in the Asian diet, thereby resulting in hoarding and potentially increasing the inflation rate. Such scenarios will provide lots of investment opportunities. Things are often not as clear as it seems at first, but for those who have practiced second-level thinking, they will be able to identify them. These people are not susceptible to the usual phenomenon of group-think, and thus more likely to outperform. For those who are interested, try understanding how John Paulson, Founder and President of Paulson and Co, a renowned hedge fund, made billions shortselling sub-prime mortgages in 2007, and subsequently making more billions investing in gold; or we can also try to understand why some invested in US real estate in 2007 and tolerated 5 long years of real-estate correction before succumbing in 2012 just before the recovery begins to take shape. It is also amazing to examine why Stephen Schwarzman of Blackstone guided his company to start buying properties from foreclosure in end 2011 and early 2012 because of his vision that the continual growth in population and demographics, along with the progress in immigration reform will likely revive the industry. Of course, astute readers will quickly point out that Paulson, in the early example, has also lost a lot of money when Gold prices collapsed intermittently in 2012/13, but it just serves to substantiate my point that the inter-relationship between different factors are dynamic, and we have to continuously practice and hone this second-level thinking.

In essence, second-level thinking is a pre-requisite for any good scenario-planning exercises. And scenario-planning is all about providing different overlays to a basic view. Adopting this "what-if" mindset is important, and it comes from experience. As Will Rogers, the famous American comedian and performer once said,

> *"Good judgment comes from experience,*
> *and a lot of that comes from bad judgment."*

It is through sheer practice that one hones the art of thinking. Helicopter-frameworks help to focus on the material variables, whereas appropriate comparison lends further conviction to the view, but scenario-planning is really about developing wisdom from experience, along with a bit of imagination.

Of course, when Howard Marks talks about "second-level" thinking, he cannot possibly be just referring to just the second level of thinking. Good analysts or investors form views by considering several derivatives of a particular event, ie developing several overlays on top of the basic view.

"There are known knowns, that is, there are things we know that we know. There are known unknowns; that is to say, there are things that we now know we don't know. But there are also unknown unknowns – there are things we do not know we don't know."

~United States Secretary of Defense,
Donald Rumsfeld, 2002

I believe that Mr Rumsfeld summed it up ideally when he talked about the "knowns" and "unknowns". Forming views with overlays, like scenario-planning in the military context is about dealing with "knowns" and "unknowns". Sophisticated analysts and investors harness the experiences of different groups of people from different fields to build the overlays, in order to derive fresh insights.

A few examples of the types of overlays in the business and investment fields include:

- Demographic pattern changes
- Business and investment cycles
- Commodity prices and cycles
- Foreign exchange movements
- Geopolitical developments
- Technological and innovation disruptions

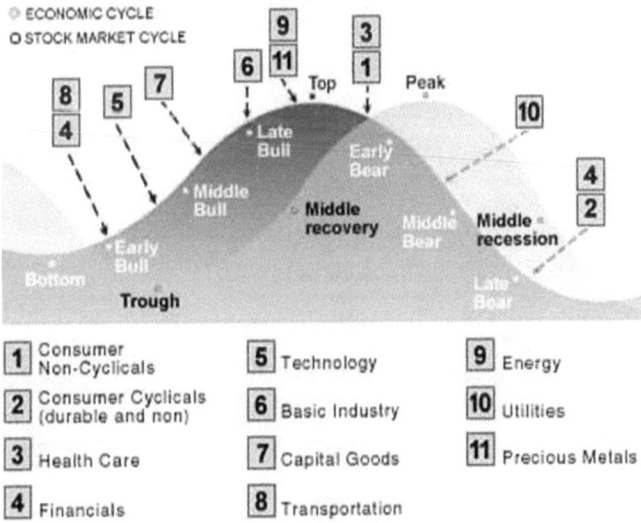

Source: ygraph.com/graphs/businesscycle

And each type of overlay has its respective helicopter-frameworks and suitable comp-set for us to form views. And overlaying them on top of one another often generates more new insights. The risk we will face in the future is more uni-dimensional thinking, accentuated by the mainstream 24/7 news-cycle. This will distract us further from forming clear views, and the duty is ours, to hone our skills further through constant curiosity and imagination.

6 CONNECTING THE DOTS

You can't connect the dots looking forward, you can only connect them looking backwards. So you have to trust that the dots will somehow connect in your future. You have to trust in something: your gut, destiny, life, karma, whatever. Because believing that the dots will connect down the road will give you the confidence to follow your heart, even when it leads you off the well-worn path.

~ Steve Jobs, 2005

Visionary ex-CEO of Apple, Inc

Brain development refers to the process of creating, removing or strengthening connections among the neurons. A neuron or nerve cell is an electrically excitable cell that processes and transmits information through electrical and chemical signals and the connections made among the neurons are called synapses. Synapses organize the brain by forming pathways that connect the parts of the brain governing everything we do, from simple tasks that we take for granted like breathing and sleeping to complex deliberate activities like thinking and feeling. This is the essence of postnatal brain development, because at birth, very few synapses have been formed. The synapses present at birth governs our basic bodily functions but the development of synapses occurs at an astounding rate during a baby's early years. According to the US Dept of Health and Human Services, the cerebral cortex of a healthy toddler may create 2 million synapses per second at its peak. When a child reach three years old, their brains have approximately 1 quadrillion (or 1,000 trillion/1 million billion!) synapses, many more than they will ever need. Some of these synapses are strengthened or remain intact over the growing years, but many are gradually discarded. This process of synapse elimination—or pruning—is a normal part of development. According to the research, approximately 50% the synapses formed at that point of time would have been discarded by the time a child reach adolescence, leaving the number they will have for most of the rest of their lives. The development of the brain continues throughout the lifespan of a human, continuously strengthening. Therefore the wise adage "Life is a continuously-learning journey" is right all along.

In a certain way, connecting-the-dots is similar to the

process of establishing synapses between neurons. Many of the synapses were eliminated because of a lack of use and strengthening, just like how we lost much knowledge and experience we pick up over our growing years. I remembered listening to Steve Jobs during his famous 2005 commencement speech at Stanford University, about how his decision to drop-out of college led him to take up a course that he was interested in at that point of time – "calligraphy instruction". During the class, he learned about serif and san serif typefaces, and about varying the amount of space between different letter combinations, and what makes great typography great. As he described, "It was beautiful, historical, artistically subtle in a way that science can't capture, and I found it fascinating." This apparently unrelated interest led him to design and develop multiple typefaces or proportionally spaced fonts for Apple's first Macintosh computer. When the Macintosh was introduced, it was the first computer with beautiful typography.

It was an inspiring moment for me to hear that from the legendary Steve Jobs as well, because I now see how important it is to treat the pursuit of all things and interests seriously, because you will never know what knowledge or wisdom you gather today may come to be useful in the future. In an age of ubiquitous access to information via mobile smart devices, it is crucial to be exposed to as many disciplines, in order to connect-the-dots.

Insanity is doing the same thing over and over again and expecting different results.

~ Albert Einstein

Imagination requires both knowledge and wisdom. There is a difference, and I shall illustrate this with a story I've heard from an entrepreneurial thought leader.

There was an intelligent student from China who had the fortune to be admitted into an Ivy-league university in the US to pursue his higher education. He completed his doctorate degree and went back to his small village to visit his family, and not unexpectedly, he had a lot of pride as he basked in the glory and attention that his family and kin showered on him. One fine morning, as he was strolling on the farm, he saw an old farmer watering his plants. This farmer recognized him but did not greet him, and this young man felt slighted. He walked over and challenged the old farmer. "Hey there, didn't you see me? I am the pride of this village, and I am a top student from a top-tier university in the US. I challenge you to a contest – Ask me any question and if I cannot answer you, I will give you a hundred bucks. And I will ask you a question, if you cannot answer, you have to give me a hundred bucks!" The farmer looked up at him, slightly irritated and said "I have neither the time nor a hundred bucks to give you if I lose". The young man, not wanting to back down, proudly declared, "I figured so too, you poor farmer. Well, if you cannot answer my question, you only have to pay me a buck. How's that?" The farmer thought for a while, and finding it quite a good deal, he agreed to it. Feeling confident, the young man continued, "Since you are the country bumpkin, I shall let you ask me a question first" The farmer paused a while and asked, "What animal climbs up a mountain with 4 legs, sleeps on the mountain with 2 legs, and climbs down the mountain with 3 legs?" The young man was stunned. He wrecked his head to think of an answer but cannot seem to find a logical one. In the end, he forked out a hundred dollar bill from his pocket and declared, "Alright, I lost, I don't know the answer." The old farmer took the money, and walked away. The young man was shocked and exasperated, "Hey, old man, what's the answer?" The old man stared blankly at him and said, "Oh, I don't know". With that, he forked out a dollar coin from his pocket and passed it to the young man, before walking off with a smirk on his face.

As you can tell, there is a real difference between knowledge and wisdom. Einstein once said that "Wisdom is not a product of schooling but of the lifelong attempt to acquire it". Lifelong curiosity is important to keep the brain active and the strengthening of synapses. We must continue to learn different disciplines and avoid the pitfall of staying within our comfort zone with respect to the acquisition of knowledge. And with experience, one can develop wisdom. The mind is a sophisticated and wonderful thing, and there are limitless things we can achieve if we set our mind to lifelong-imagining, no pun intended.

Constant imagination will aid one in his/her efforts to develop overlays on top of the basic views. A good example is illustrated in Michael Maubossin's 2006 book entitled "More Than You Know - Finding Financial Wisdom in Unconventional Places". In it, he explained how the study of social insects and their behavior provides more insights into market behavior than any financial theory does. In fact, he recounts how recent research highlighted surprisingly, that people without particular expertise can collectively solve problems that stump experts. This research was also substantiated in James Surowiecki classic book, "The Wisdom of Crowds", and one of the main reasons is essentially the diversity of views and perspectives that result in an ever more accurate approximation in a complex scenario. Views formed by the multi-disciplinary overlays often ends up more accurate than uni-dimensional views.

Michael used ants as an example of puny insects with the extraordinary ability to perform tasks of solving complex problems such as optimizing the location of a food source, ie a trash heap and the colony by instinct, not by math. Ants are shaped by nature to exploit the wonders of diversity and develop a collective habitat around it. He notes that an ant colony tolerates inefficiency, noise and random running around because that ensures that it finds new food sources. Similarly, bees also exhibit high propensity to perform complex tasks and resolve difficult challenges. When a worker bee returns to the hive, it dances to tell the colony that it has found food and where the food is, with the length of the dance determining how much the colony needs that kind of resource. He highlighted that social insects do not rely on any central direction or commander, because they function well under a decentralized model. However, such decentralization doesn't imply chaos as these individual insects can still work collectively to ensure the habitat or colony's sustained survival.

We can all learn a lesson from the ants and bees, that is, the collective behavior of individuals who work independently may very well be more powerful than the advice of the experts. Now, I can empathize with the reader – Why are we talking about listening to a crowd of independent non-experts, especially in a book supposedly teaching one how to think and form expert views? The answer lies in the humbling understanding and acceptance that learning is a lifelong journey, and we can always learn something from somebody. Only constant curiosity and an earnest desire to enrich oneself, can we be able to develop good overlays for forming ever better views.

In the context of an investment world, the market can be seen as an ant colony or a bee hive, with individuals and institutions working without central direction and drawing on various sources of information to derive a range of values for a variety of commodities and "products". This contributes a lot to another wise old adage,

"Don't blame the market as the market is always right!"

Niall Ferguson's classic bible on Capitalism, "The Ascent of Money" highlighted several historical occasions where crowds sometimes went from manic depressions to irrational exuberance in different markets especially when investors stop behaving as independent, diverse agents and begin acting in concert. These episodes used to be rare, but they have severe and wide consequences. Advancement in global connectivity has increased the correlation of different asset classes and geographies through the prevalence of derivative instruments (though the irony is that these instruments are designed with the noble goal of diversifying risks), and improvement in communications technologies and mass media will only seek to accentuate the speed and impact of herd behavior.

There has already been a growing interest in this area, and a relatively new field known as behavioral economics and behavioral finance is a common staple in several business school curriculums. Behavioral economics and its related field, behavioral finance, study the effects of social, cognitive, and emotional factors on the economic decisions of individuals and institutions and the consequences for market prices, returns, and the resource allocation. Connecting different dots together, behavioral models typically integrate insights from psychology with neo-classical economic theory with three prevalent themes, according to behavioral finance scholar, Hersh Shefrin:

- **Heuristics**: People often make decisions based on approximate rules of thumb and not strict logic

- **Framing**: The collection of anecdotes and stereotypes that make up the mental emotional filters individuals rely on to understand and respond to events

- **Market inefficiencies**: These include mis-pricings and non-rational decision making

As this is not a psychology or behavioral science textbook to expound on the wide plethora of human biases and the various forms of heuristics, I will not dwell too much in this area, but suffice to say, understanding the various aspects of behavioral finance, just like studying the behavior of social insects, is a good way to develop the ability to build useful overlays in our journey to form good views.

Investing and doing business has much in common with art; they all require intuitive and flexible approaches. Holbrook Jackson, a well-known English bookworm of the early 20th century once said, "Intuition is reason in a hurry" and there is nothing wrong with intuition. We are in need of intuition more than ever. However, intuition is the ability to form views because of the synapses or "connections" between the neurons or "dots" that one have developed in his brain. Malcolm Gladwell, in one of his bestsellers, "Blink", highlighted the importance of intuition, and argues that intuitive judgment is developed through experience, training, and knowledge. He raised several examples such as the Getty Kuoros, the Cleveland firemen and the Pepsi Challenge to substantiate the point. In my experience, the corporate thought leaders are often those who internalize the vast experience and exposure they have, and synthesize them into useful anecdotes and actionable strategies. They tend to be good story-tellers who seem to operate a lot by intuition, and their actions are usually justified by those anecdotes. More often than not, we are surprised at how accurate they turn out to be. Science is currently still too nascent to fully explain such phenomena as intuition but the corporate and investment world values it. They just call it slightly differently and more elegantly – experience.

Since I began this chapter with a quote from the late business legend, Steve Jobs, I find it most apt to close it with another quote from the same speech that inspire this writer deeply. He ended his speech with an advice to the graduating students of Stanford to "Stay Hungry, Stay Foolish". For those who hear it for the first time, they might find it odd but there is truly a lot of wisdom in this piece of advice. In the hustle and bustle of modern life, there are just so many things that bombard us and so much that demands of our attention. Yet, many on the path lost patience, and gave up pursuing new knowledge because they felt jerked around by the wide plethora of stuff. Sometimes, we may feel foolish for pursuing seemingly useless disciplines, but only to realize years later that it can be put to good use. The best attitude, as Steve Jobs alluded to, is to maintain a "hungry and foolish" but earnest countenance towards all that we have embarked to learn, and stay the course in having the faith that somehow the dots will connect in the future.

7 CATALYSTS

There is a tide in the affairs of men,
Which taken at the flood, leads on to fortune.
Omitted, all the voyage of their life is bound in shallows and in
miseries. On such a full sea are we now afloat. And we must
take the current when it serves, or lose our ventures ~Brutus

~ William Shakespeare, Julius Caesar Act 4

So far, we have been talking about the importance of forming views in the most effective and efficient ways. However, views are only appreciated if they are proven credible over an extended period of time. This is often apparent in the corporate world. Consider the following scenario: A sophomore from a local university just got an internship in an investment firm. He just completed his basic business school modules, comprising mainly of accounting 101 and corporate finance 101. Armed with these basic skillset, he joyfully started work in the firm. On his first week of internship, he was asked to analyze companies' earnings per share because it happened to be the quarterly earnings release season. The intern was puzzled and made a comment, "Shouldn't we be focusing on Return on Equity" instead of the "Earnings per share"? His supervisor heard this and gave him an earful, reprimanding him for being "lazy" and shirking work, thus finding reasons not to proceed with the analysis. That very same day happened to be Berkshire Hathaway's annual shareholder meeting, and both the supervisor and the intern ("Wow, what a lucky intern to be able to attend the popular shareholder meeting - highly unlikely but let's just assume it happened!") listened attentively to legendary investor, Chairman & CEO of Berkshire Hathaway, Warren Buffett's comments. Halfway through the CEO's address, Warren Buffett highlighted, "These days, many investors and managers focused on the earnings per share, and get so worked up when companies' management failed to meet the analysts' expectations of the earnings per share (EPS). They often over-react to these numbers which are mostly irrelevant. What one should focus on is the Return on Equity (RoE)...." At this point, the intern turned around to look at his supervisor, who was nodding intently at every word that this Oracle of Omaha is saying, apparently not realizing the puzzled look the intern was wearing on his face.

How often do we see the same message spoken by different people, having materially different impact? We may conclude that this is irrational, but this is precisely why it is important to see through the hypocrisy and filter the key messages from the noise. For a corporate greenhorn, the ability to form view is half the battle won, but developing credibility attached to these views is equally important. I am not saying in the aforementioned example that the intern is 100% right or that the supervisor has no basis for insisting the intern to analyze quarterly earnings per share figures. In fact, having worked in the investment world for the last decade, I am fully cognizant of how and why the intern need to do to perform the analysis competently, but the point here is really the credentials attached to the intern who made that comment, as opposed to the very same comment made by the 82-year-old Sage of Omaha.

Now, knowing the irrationality of it all, we can spend all our time arguing whether is this fair or not, or as a mentor of mine once said, "You can instead choose to spend your energies building credibility". And all these years, I have set off to accomplish exactly just that, and in this chapter, I like to highlight one very important aspect of establishing credibility in your views -

Catalysts

The time dimension in establishing views is often not highlighted enough. Everyone can form views that will be accurate some of the times. For example, if someone tells you that someday, we will all die. Will you consider this person an oracle or a good seer? I would hardly think so, because as the wise adage goes, "Even a broken clock is right twice a day. Quoting something as certain as death (or tax, for that matter) is definitely not considered good forecasting or forming a useful view. It should be noted that there are many doomsayers in the world across all ages and cultures, from the Mayans[10] who forecasted the

---

[10] To be fair, the Mayans did not forecast the end of the world on the 21 Dec 2012. Professional Mayanist scholars had indicated that there were no Mayan accounts that forecasted impending doom on a global scale. Given that there must be an end date to which the Long Count calendar of the "precision-freakish" Mayans must stop at, it is not unreasonable to stop the calendar on the 21 Dec 2012, which is effectively the end-date of a 5,126 year long cycle in the

21 Dec 2012 apocalypse to Nostradamus of the 16th century to Harold Camping, the President of Family Radio, a California-based radio station, who forecasted that Jesus would return on 21 May 2011 and initiate the Rapture that would occur on the 21 October 2011. Despite wrongly predicting that Judgment Day would occur on 6 September 1994, it was truly amazing to read and hear stories of people still believing in him, consequently selling and donating their entire fortune to prepare for the Rapture event, which did not materialize on the said date.

Moving on from the world of esoteric predictions to the world of investments and business, it is noteworthy to mention the various personalities that have gained much fame due to their foresight prior to the Global Financial Crisis (GFC) of 2008. Some were investment managers such as John Paulson, Peter Schiff, Steve Eisman and Dr Michael Burry[11]. Others were famous economists like

---

Mesoamerican Long Count calendar. However, the imagination of many people has led to the wrongful interpretation of this date as the End of Times, though a movie buff like I, would have it to thank for the visually-stunning and highly entertaining blockbuster movie, 2012, starring John Cusack.

[11] Steve Eisman's and Dr Michael Burry's stories are well-documented in Michael Lewis classic book "The Big Short",

Nouriel Roubini, and strategists and celebrity-analysts like Med Jones and Meredith Whitney. The website, http://www.economicpredictions.org/who-predicted-the-financial-crisis.htm presented a good comparative prediction table showing prediction statements, dates, and references made by Dean Baker, Med Jones, Peter Schiff and Nouriel Roubini. However, these people did not enjoy the positive limelight on the very first day that they made such forecasts. For much of 2005-2007, most of the aforementioned were ostracized and labeled as lunatics, despite them producing tons of substantive evidence and research to back their views. We humans, have a natural bias towards denial, and Michael Lewis's book "The Big Short" underscored the interesting anecdotes of how clients continued to shun Steve Eisman and Dr Michael Burry despite being vindicated within a span of 3 years. The main idea behind timing is to achieve what Meredith Whitney did back in 2007, when she was working as a senior banking analyst of Oppenheimer & Co. In October 2007, Meredith Whitney wrote a pessimistic research report on Citigroup which stated that, the bank, badly hit by the subprime market meltdown, was undercapitalized

---

which illustrated their painstaking journey of being labelled as anti-social misfits despite being extremely right, and profited tremendously from the subprime crisis.

despite its huge size, predicting that asset sale or dividend cut is required to stabilize the situation, thus downgrading the stock. She was proven right and was consequently celebrated as an Oracle of Wall Street, and that report landed her on the cover of the 18 August 2008 issue of Fortune magazine[12].

What is amazing is also how wrong some famous economic and business icons were. Ben Bernanke and his predecessor, Alan Greenspan made several statements, highlighting how the financial crisis caught everyone by surprise and was "a once-in-a-century event" whose consequences proved far more devastating than had been widely expected and that "We all misjudged the risks involved. Everybody missed it - academia, the Federal Reserve, all regulators." Well, this writer, for one, does not believe that the Federal Reserve Chiefs truly meant what they say. In the climate of uncertainty and panic, apology and feigning ignorance seems the most politically-

---

[12] Of course, as with many prior examples, Meredith Whitney also made a few bad calls after that. Her highly convicted prediction that the municipal-bond market was set for an epic implosion in 2010 did not materialize simply because the federal and state authorities are not static agents but dynamic variables who will react accordingly as well. In fact, the municipal bond market certainly has her and other doomsayers to thank for averting a major collapse.

palatable approach, but another infamous individual's account seems to be more accurate. Chuck Prince, former CEO of Citigroup once said that Citigroup's commitment to leveraged buy-out deals despite fears of reduced liquidity because of the occurring sub-prime meltdown is simple:

"As long as the music is playing, you've got to get up and dance."

George Soros, another legendary investor who broke the Bank of England back in 16 September 1992 otherwise known Black Wednesday or the day that speculators (George Soros was the leader of the pack) broke the pound[13], also acquired a stake in Lehman Brothers, which became an infamous casualty in the GFC of 2008. The key point here is Timing and it is an elusive topic. Judgment calls are made every single day, and the only way to build credibility with your views is to overlay the timing element with the process of forming views. Goldman Sachs became the winner among its investment banking peers because of their ability to time it better than anyone

---

[13] The speculators did not actually break the Bank of England, but they forced the British government to pull it from the European Exchange Rate Mechanism (ERM), because it became quite apparent that it was losing billions trying to buoy its currency artificially.

else on Wall Street. While I am not going to argue about the morality issues and the decline in the level of trust between the bank and its clients, which are already well covered and debated on various newspapers and media, it was undeniable that Goldman Sach's ability to time and execute their exit from the subprime mortgage and other collateralized debt obligation positions was impressive.

For example, if someone said today that the United States current debt level is unsustainable, many of us will be saying, "Duh? So? Aren't you stating the obvious?" In today's sound-bite media age, it is no longer enough to know the headlines of the day, but rather to identify which are the catalysts that will trigger the chain of events from happening.

Traditionally used in Chemistry, catalysts are something that initiate or cause an important event to occur. In the area of Finance and investments, it is also similar – a catalyst are event that result in another event or a series of events. A catalyst can be both positive or negative, and a positive catalyst can be a positive earnings report or a regulatory change that will boost a certain industry relative to others. The converse is also true for a negative catalyst. For example, CNBC's Rick Santelli noted recently, "We are in our sixth year since the US officially went into recession and yet, we are still in crisis management mode." The holy grail in the world of investments and business today is to identify the day that the Fed will begin to remove its mega liquidity pipe from the market. This catalyst for a sizeable market correction could come in the form of a "posturing" statement from the Federal Reserve, or a rate hike, or it could come in the form of other measures. When the "posturing" statement or a particular measure was implemented, the market will react, often in a knee-jerked way, but sometimes, it can achieve the goal of making the politicians capitulate, despite the market comprising of so many discrete individual agents. We have seen several episodes of how bond traders managed to force European politicians succumb to agreeing to massive bailout of their neighbors between 2009-2012. However, it is worthwhile to note that Rick also famously exclaimed that "there is no expiration date on faulty illogical ideas," as he expects any Fed exit to be "very, very messy." And at the end of the day, when the Fed decides to exit, they will not be able to put the "liquidity toothpaste back in the tube." In this case, if the reader, like Rick, does not believe in the efficacy of Quantitative Easing and loose monetary policies, then, the view would be that the impact post a signaling will be substantial, and the prevalence of high-frequency trading and other forms of algorithmic trading will only seek to accentuate the amplitude of the boom and bust cycles. Just for fun, a second-level thinker and practitioner should also consider the prospects that the Ben Bernanke and the Federal Reserve are not static beings, but dynamically receiving the messages from the public, so whether will the Federal Reserve capitulate or will he adopt a determined stance like Paul Volcker in the 1970s and 80s, in his epic battle against inflation, is another judgment call.

Of course, identifying catalysts for macro views is important and interesting, but I caution against falling into the vanity trap of getting lost in it. Forming macro views allow us to pit our logic against the well-known thought leaders, but seldom do these views result in any actionable opportunities because the views encompass too many dynamic variables. The vanity trap in this context refers to our inherent desire to feel important and engaged intellectually with the corporate titans of today. A good analyst and investor must be able to identify catalysts for micro-analysis as well. This is because, identifying such catalysts will be highly rewarding and profitable, because the opportunities can materialize in relatively more specific ways. There are different types of catalysts to focus on. It is not the aim of this book to list down all the kind of catalysts, but I wish to reiterate a couple broad varieties of catalysts for readers which I have mentioned in prior chapters, to explore further.

- Identify stress points via leverage analysis – This was highlighted in the chapter illustrating the Equity Multiplier within the Helicopter Framework – Dupont analysis. Many books on investments focus on teaching readers on identifying companies which are well-performing because they are targeted at retail investors looking for investments in the public markets. This is all good and appropriate, but in the world of business and institutional investments, it is important to recognize that the analysis is not as simple and straightforward as what was elaborated in these books. Companies which are well-performing across cycles and cash-rich do not need the capital from investors if they are generating positive cash-flow from their operations. Identify the timing for refinancing or expansion plans, overlaying them with the interest rate cycles, would provide new insights and interesting views to act upon.

- Identify events that will trigger the supply chain disruptions and plan for subsequent scenarios. Technology advancements and information access has truly revolutionized various business processes, as imaginative and bold individuals enter the world of investments and business, they are breaking new boundaries every day. I remembered a movie scene from the 2010 award winning movie, "The Social Network" where Mark Zuckerberg, portrayed by the talented Jesse Eisenberg telling his (ex)-girlfriend, how his pal, Eduardo Saverin made US$300,000 betting oil futures one summer during an internship, simply because he likes meteorology which helps in predicting the weather, consequently able to find the correlating pattern of predicting price of heating oil. While this came from a Hollywood script, many traders will tell you that this is actually quite common in the industry. Good analysts triangulate data from different sources to perform good scenario planning and identify the specific catalysts especially in the commodities market. I am aware of good investors (traders) who tie up with the geologists to identify and quantify impact of foreseeable natural disasters in order to identify the stress points so as to time their entry and exit.

- Identify key individuals or institutions that are stakeholders – This sort of analysis is known commonly in the field of investments as stakeholder, or more narrowly, shareholder analysis. As globalization and increasing urbanization occurs, the middle income group has grown significantly in several emerging markets. It is not uncommon that as young man and woman in these markets scale the Maslow Hierarchy of needs[14] due to growing affluence (Refer to Appendix for a pictorial representation of the 5 levels defined by Maslow), they strive for different purposes and meaning in their life. The reality is that many rich tycoons in Latin America and Asia are finding it difficult to compel their children to take over their family businesses because the succeeding generation are finding fulfillment in a different way beyond materialistic

---

[14] Maslow Hierarchy of Needs is a theory in psychology proposed by Abraham Maslow in his 1943 paper "A Theory of Human Motivation".

pursuits. These creates a variety of opportunities for private bankers and smart investors. As people choose to exit from their businesses, identifying and analyzing who are the natural and potential successors as well as the extent of compatibility can serve as good catalysts for particular outcomes.

These are but just some examples of how one can identify catalysts for his/her views. It is an evolving and continuous journey, because the skill of forming views is more an Art than a precise Science. Before I end this chapter, I would however like to highlight a very good piece of advice from George Soros, who highlighted in his seminal 1994 book, The Alchemy of Finance:

"Perception is not reality but a market participant's perception shapes the reality, which in turn shapes the market participant's perception"

In essence, the concept of reflexivity, which highlights how market participants' actions and thoughts shape the market facts and reality, indicate the dynamic nature of the principal agents of a market, and in forming views, it is always wise to consider the inter-relationship.

He also underscored that history does not move from outcome to outcome but rather from expectation to outcome to expectation, and that success "depends a lot on the ability to anticipate prevailing expectations:".

A wise mentor once told me that as an investor, "I cannot afford to be an optimist and pessimist, I have to be a realist." Unfortunately, it is apparent that the world often goes through what the medical world referred to as the Kübler-Ross model, or more commonly referred to as the "Five Stages of Grief"[15] across all investment and business cycles in spite of stark facts staring straight at us, primarily because we most often find ourselves stuck in the first stage - Denial, but as Kyle Bass, founder of hedge fund, Hayman Capital in Dallas, Texas said, *"It is the qualitative shift in the market participants' belief systems that literally flips a switch overnight"*

The future, indeed belongs to those who can form better and *timely* views than everyone else.

---

[15] The Five Stages of Grief has the commonly–known acronym DABDA, include: Denial, Anger, Bargaining, Depression, Acceptance.

8 CONCLUSION

Now, this is not the end. This is not even the beginning of the end.
But it is, perhaps, the end of the beginning.

- Winston Churchill,
Prime Minister of Britain

As we reach the concluding chapter of this book, I will like to once again, congratulate you on your initiative to pick up this book and finish it. The impetus to action on this journey of discovery is what separates the winners from the quitters. As the writer, I will be hypocritical to say that I do not wish for this to be a bestseller, but I recognize that the main content and key lessons from this book are more suited for those who are currently working or interested in the world of business and investments. Even within this segment of readers, there are the corporate veterans, greenhorns or those who have some level of experience. Therefore, I try to be balanced in my approach, with some form of guidance to the corporate greenhorns and those fresh out of colleges as well as encouraging anecdotes and some refreshing nuggets of wisdom for the more experienced readers. The guidance in the form of the pair of shoes (Usage of Frameworks + Relativity Mindset) may seem elementary to some, but it is always good to remind ourselves the importance of personal humility especially in the field of investments, and that this journey of forming good views require the consistent and inquisitive practice. Many global thought leaders use formulas as initial basis to form views, and I have highlighted how Return-on-Capital which Joel Greenblatt introduced, and the corresponding subset (Return-on-Equity) which Warren Buffett emphasized repeatedly to be a good starting point. The Dupont analysis is thus one example of a helicopter framework derived from the ROE formula. I have also listened to smart fund managers like Kyle Bass, utilizing the traditional Equation of Exchange[16],

---

[16] The Equation of Exchange, in Monetary Economics – Quantity Theory of Money is defined as the following:

$M * V = P * Q$, to form succinct and clear actionable views about modern monetary policies such as Quantitative Easing. We will learn from these thought leaders that equations and formulas are very useful foundations to develop our own helicopter frameworks.

For those who are slightly more experienced, you may find that the topics on Overlays, Connecting-the-dots, and Catalysts interesting. These are advanced topics in the realm of Forming Views, and as I alluded to in the description of myself, I am a mere apprentice on this journey of improving my skills to form views as well. The intent of this book is to ignite the interest of the readers to explore further and make the discoveries themselves, and to perhaps share those ideas with me as we improve ourselves collectively. (i.e. ideas for future books?) It would be interesting to note that after reading this book, one may look at the world differently as we will begin to

---

$M * V = P * Q$ where, for a given period,

M is the total nominal amount of money in circulation on average in an economy.
Q is the velocity of money, that is the average frequency with which a unit of money is spent.
P is the price level &
Q is an index of real expenditures (on newly produced goods and services).

identify how thought leaders think as we evaluate their narratives. As Tom Brokaw, an iconic American television journalist, anchor and managing editor of NBC Nightly News from 1982 to 2004, said during a recent interview, *"Journalism needs to get in front of technology, and not be led by them"*, else the negative ramification of that will be a substantial drop in the quality of the narrative as we get distracted by too much noise.

Amidst the chaos and the many obligations that demand our intention, it is easy to lose ourselves, and we begin to question the existential meaning of what we do. However, having gone through similar struggles, I like to share an inspiring story to those who currently face challenges and difficulties in what they do:

Many years ago during the age of the Warring States in China, there was a General who had fought in countless battles, and came so close to death numerous times. Despite being a successful military commander, he often craved for the moments where he immersed himself in the heat of the battle. Ironically, he found a sense of peace in those moments, where his only focus is at the individual enemy he is targeting. He was calm and poised, with absolute determination and purpose during those moments, in spite of the seeming chaos. Once, after the end of a successful campaign with a neighboring state, the General was handsomely rewarded by the feudal lord, and he retired to his hometown for a happy reunion with his family. One fine day, as he was visiting a room housing the collection of treasures that was given to him, either from the feudal lord or from the spoils of the successful campaign, he came across a shelf of antique vases with elaborate designs and patterns. As he picked up one especial vase, and admired at the beauty of its designs, he accidentally lost his footings, and almost dropped the vase. The General was exasperated, and had an episode of what we would now call, a panic attack. As sweat began to pour out of his forehead, he sat down on a chair and heaved a sigh of relief. At this moment, the General had an epiphany – For all his life, he has countless brushes with Death itself, but there was never a time where he felt as nervous as that very moment. What was this vase to him that can match even his life? He was suddenly enlightened, and with a smile, he dropped the vase in his hand, breaking it.

If you found it almost ridiculous that the General would break a good beautiful vase for nothing, then you are not alone. I felt that too after I listened to this story, but on further introspection, this is a very meaningful tale that we can draw lessons on. Many of us have faced countless difficulties and challenges in our lives, some of which most of us cannot even remember. For example, can you imagine the neo-natal shock that all of us face when we came into the world from our mothers' wombs? As fetuses, we do not use our lungs as they are not functional and the pulmonary circulation does not operate. The fetus obtains oxygen and nutrients from the mother through the placenta and the umbilical cord. However, when we first came out into this world and drew in our first breathe, imagine the shock we have faced at that point of time?

Going through the multiple challenges of growing up, we faced daunting challenges along the way, but have always overcome to be in the position today, reading this very book. The impermanence nature of worldly things dictate that our challenges and "perceived sufferings" will too, pass. As with the General, it is often our attachment to certain assumptions or imagined future that causes us much misery. Therefore, we must always reexamine our assumptions and adopt the demeanor of the General when he is facing life-and-death moments during battle – facing the tasks at hand with determined focus and attention. As

Will Smith in the 2013 movie, "After Earth" said to his son, *"Don't get me wrong. Danger is real, but Fear is a Choice"*.

I wish you all the success in your endeavours.

9 APPENDIX

5-STEP DUPONT ANALYSIS

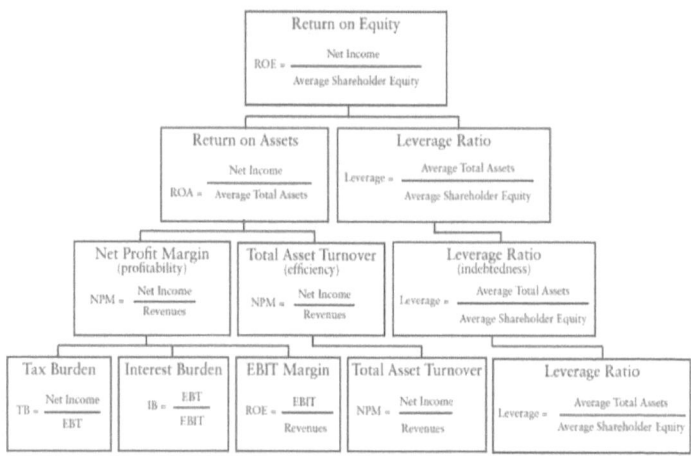

Another example of a Helicopter Framework – Total Shareholder Returns

Source: Boston Consulting Group

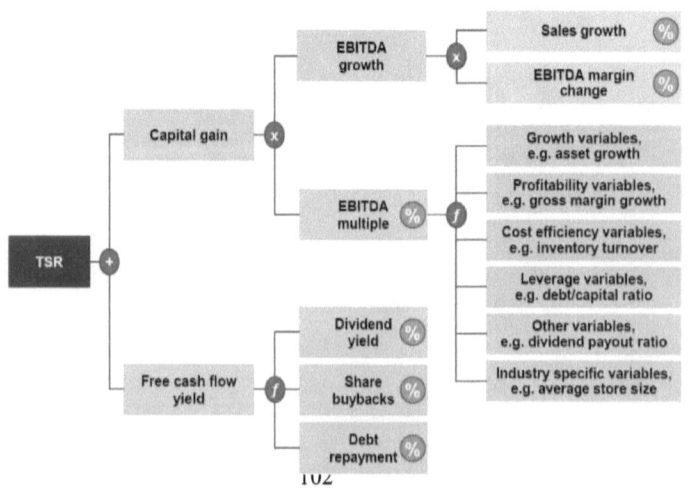

Maslow's Hierarchy of Needs

Source: Mazlow's Hierarchy of Needs.svg

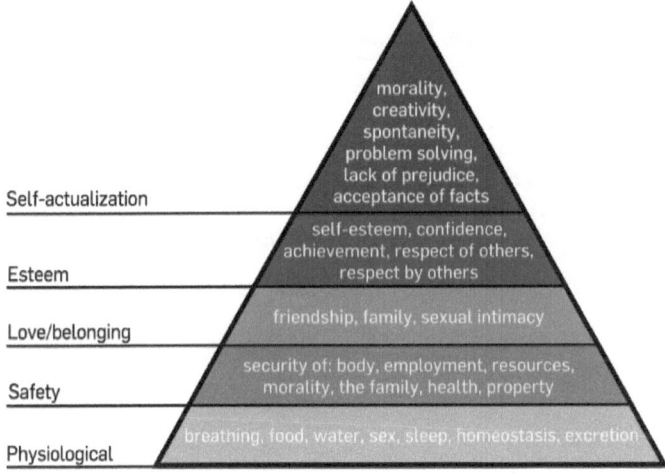

10 BIBLIOGRAPHY

1. W. Chan Kim and Renée Mauborgne, Blue Ocean Strategy: How to Create Uncontested Market Space and Make Competition Irrelevant, 2005, Harvard Business School Press

2. Paul S Myers, Knowledge Management and Organizational Design (Resources for the Knowledge-Based Economy), 1996, Routledge

3. Michael J. Mauboussin, Finding Financial Wisdom in Unconventional Places, 2006, Columbia University Press

4. Howard Marks, The Most Important Thing - Uncommon Sense for the Thoughtful Investor, 2011, Columbia University Press

5. Orit Gadiesh and Hugh MacArthur, Lessons from Private Equity Any Company Can Use – Memo to the CEO, 2008, Harvard Business Press

6. Michael Lewis - The Big Short - Inside the Doomsday Machine, 2010, W.W.Norton & Co

7. Andrew Ross Sorkin, Too Big to Fail: The Inside Story of How Wall Street and Washington Fought to Save the Financial System—and Themselves, 2009 Viking Press

8. Richard Bernstein, Navigate the Noise: Investing with One of Wall Street's Top Investment Strategists, 2001, Wiley Publishing

9. Daniel R. Solin, The Smartest Investment Book You'll Ever Read - The Simple, Stress-Free Way to Reach Your Investment Goals, 2006, Perigee, Penguin Publishing

10. Ha-Joon Chang, 23 Things They Don't Tell You About Capitalism, 2011, Bloomsbury Press

11. Seth A. Klarman, Margin of Safety: Risk-Averse Value Investing Strategies for the Thoughtful Investor, 1991, HarperCollins Canada, Limited

12. George Soros, The Alchemy of Finance, 1994, John Wiley & Sons, Inc

13. Peter Lynch, One Up On Wall Street: How To Use What You Already Know To Make Money In The Market, 2000, Fireside - Simon & Schuster

14. Benjamin Graham, The Intelligent Investor: The Definitive Book on Value Investing. A Book of Practical Counsel (Revised Edition), 2006, HarpersCollins Publishers

15. Maria Bartiromo, Use the News: How To Separate the Noise from the Investment Nuggets and Make Money in Any Economy, 2002, HarpersCollins Publishers

16. Philip A. Fisher, Common Stocks and Uncommon

Profits and Other Writings, 1996 Wiley Investment Classics

17. Lawrence A. Cunningham, The Essays of Warren Buffett: Lessons for Investors and Managers, 2009, Carolina Academic Press

18. Joel Geenblatt, The Little Book That Still Beats the Market, 2010, John Wiley and Sons

19. Joel Greenblatt, The Big Secret for the Small Investor: A New Route to Long-Term Investment Success, 2011, Crown Publishing Group

20. Robert I. Webb, Trading Catalysts – How Events Move Markets and Create Trading Opportunities, 2007, Pearson Education Inc, FT Press

21. Howard M. Schilit & Jeremy Perler, Financial Shenanigans, 2010, McGraw-Hill Publishing

22. Dzongsar Jamyang Khyentse, What Makes You Not a Buddhist, 2007, Shambhala Publications Inc

23. Bethany McLean and Joseph Nocera, All the Devils Are Here: The Hidden History of the Financial Crisis, 2010, Penguin Press

24. Thomas L. Friedman & Michael Mandelbaum, That Used to be Us – How America Fell Behind In the World It Invented and How We Can Come Back, 2012, D&M Publishers Inc

25. Dr. Farid A. Muna, The Helicopter View and Strategic

Thinking, 2010, Web Article

26. Muna, F., Seven Metaphors on Management: Tools for Managers in the Arab World, 2003, Gower Publishing

27. Flavia Cymbalista, Ph.D, How George Soros Knows What He Knows: Towards a General Theory of Reflexivity, 2003, PDF from Websource

28. Peter D. Schiff, Crash Proof: How to Profit From the Coming Economic Collapse, 2007, John Wiley & Sons

29. Peter D. Schiff, The Little Book of Bull Moves in Bear Markets: How to Keep Your Portfolio Up When the Market is Down, 2008, John Wiley & Sons

30. Michael Brown, Roger Keynes and Andrew Lumsden, The Developing Brain, 2002, Oxford University Press

31. David Price, Andrew P. Jarman, John O Mason, Peter C. Kind, Building Brains: An Introduction to Neural Development, 2011, Wiley Publishing

32. Tony Buzan, The Speed Reading Book: Read More, Learn More, Achieve More, 2009, Educational Publishers, Pearson Educational Group

33. Tony Buzan and Barry Buzan, The Mind Map Book: How to Use Radiant Thinking to Maximize Your Brain's Untapped Potential, 1996, Penguin Group

34. Dr Farid A. Muna, The Helicopter View and Strategic Thinking, 2010, Web Resource from www.meirc.com

ABOUT THE AUTHOR

The author is a non-descript individual in his thirties, who has been interested in the world of business and investments since young. He has pursued a career in investments since graduation over the last decade in a global investment house based in Asia. A fan of legendary investors such as Benjamin Graham, Warren Buffett and Peter Lynch, he is also a keen follower and student of modern investment gurus such as Barton Biggs, Kyle Bass and Howard Marks. He is indeed blessed to be given the opportunity to apply the various investment principles he learnt in his day-job. The world of business and investment, especially the Market, despite all its glamour due to the sensationalizing of Wall Street in modern media, is a humbling place, and the author prefers to be called an Apprentice as he firmly believes that there is ever so much to learn from the world of business and investments.